JOHN RUTTER

A GAELIC BLESSING

MUSIC DEPARTMENT

OXFORD
UNIVERSITY PRESS

A Gaelic Blessing

JOHN RUTTER

The original version of this piece, for SATB choir and organ, is available (RSCM order code A0001), as are other choral voicings.

OXFORD UNIVERSITY PRESS MUSIC DEPARTMENT, GREAT CLARENDON STREET, OXFORD OX2 6DP

*Both hands on the same manual.